Written by
Camille Lancaster

Illustrated by
Emma Renfroe

**For my
Coffee Drinkers
and Dog Lovers –**
Madison
Annie
Chloe
Sam
Jax
Lori

Oakie lives in a walk-up apartment over a jewelry store on
a quaint little downtown street.
He lays out on his balcony every evening when the sun is
setting and smells the most delicious smell in the world
coming from the coffee shop a few doors down.

While Mr. Parengo roasts bags of coffee beans,
Oakie soaks in the rich, earthy aroma
and dreams about his next cup.

Oakie is a dog who loves coffee.

Every morning Oakie runs through the neighborhood
with his pal, Sam.

The two of them always end their run at Parengo Coffee
for a steaming hot Pour-over
or other delicious concoctions
made by the friendly Barista.

This is Oakie's favorite part of every day.

He sits outside on the cool sidewalk and watches
the people walk in and out of the Coffee Shop
holding their little paper cups—
laughing, talking, and sharing stories.
parengo
COFFEE
Oakie loves people-watching almost as much
as he loves coffee.
114
OPEN
P C

One day as Oakie lay on his balcony breathing in the
sweet smell of coffee,
a little bird landed on his railing.

The bird was poking around in Oakie's
flowers looking
for something to eat.

Oakie asked, "Do you like coffee?"
"Birds eat worms and little bugs,
I've never tried coffee,"
tweeted the bird as he plucked a bug
off a leaf and flew away.

"How could you live without coffee?!"
thought Oakie.

His belly was still warm from
this morning's hot, foamy
Cappuccino and he
couldn't imagine
life without coffee.

The next day, Oakie was playing in the park and ran by a squirrel sitting on the picnic table. The squirrel was nibbling on an acorn.

"Wow," said Oakie. "How can you make it through a hot summer day without a Cold Brew?"
he muttered to himself
and then plopped down in the soft, cool grass.

That night, the sly cat
who lives in the alley
was sitting in Oakie's window sill.

Oakie leaned close and watched
the cat lick the stale cupcake
she had pulled out of the dumpster.

"Yuck," said Oakie,
a little louder than he intended.

"Not yuck at all", said the cat.

Oakie was a little surprised the cat could hear him through the window.

"This is the best thing I've had all week,"
she purred then closed her eyes
and enjoyed her treat.

Oakie thought for a minute... the best thing he'd tasted that week was the delicious Lavender Iced Latte from Parengo.

It was one of their signature drinks and Oakie's absolute favorite.

The deep rich flavor of dark roasted coffee mixed with vanilla bean and a hint of lavender, swirled with creamy almond milk then served over ice was pure perfection on a warm summer evening.

Early the next morning as Oakie lay in his
warm bed dreaming about the day, 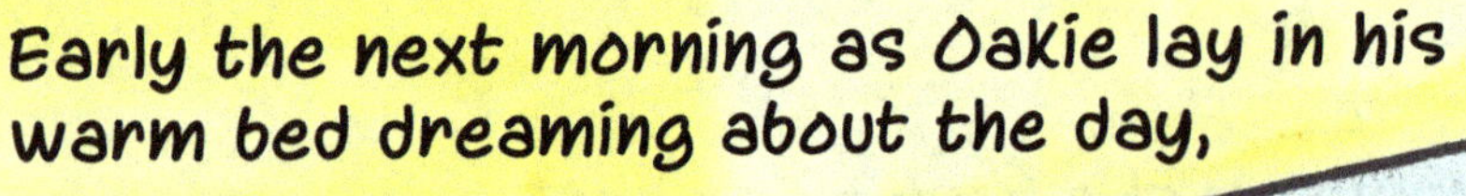 a little mouse
scampered by dragging
a big hunk of cheese.

"Wait," muttered Oakie still groggy from a
good night's sleep.

"Do you like coffee?" he asked.

"No way," squeaked the mouse. "I'm all about cheese, nuts,
grains, and a little peanut butter. Your dog food
isn't bad, but it's not my favorite,"

the mouse giggled and ran on.

"My dog food?

Has that mouse been eating
MY DOG FOOD?"
groaned Oakie to himself,
shaking the thoughts
          out of his head.

"Yuck!" he thought.

Now, Oakie couldn't wait for his morning coffee.

He was not touching that dog food today.
          Not after that sneaky ol' mouse had been in it!

Oakie rolled over on his back and stretched his legs up toward to
the ceiling with a big smile on his face dreaming about the
          Salted Carmel Latte he would order today.

          "Mmmmm, I just love coffee," he thought to himself.

Oakie's pal Sam found him still stretching
and smiling and dreaming about coffee.

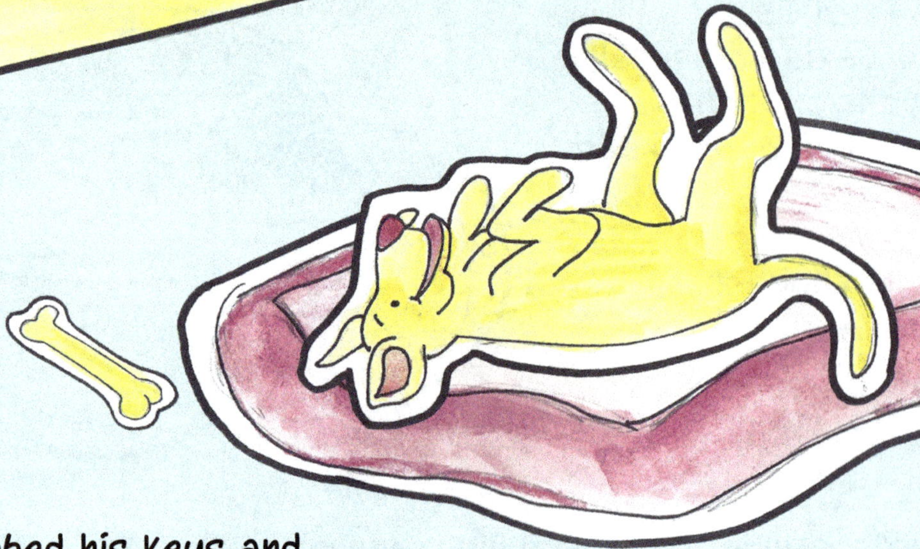

Sam grabbed his keys and
motioned for Oakie to follow him outside.

It was a beautiful morning.

The sun was shining and a cool breeze was blowing.

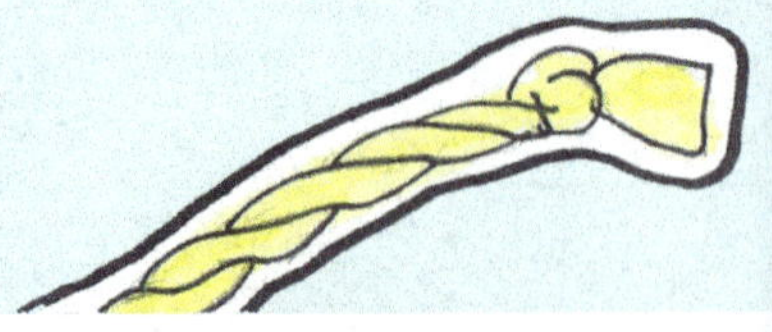

Best of all, the big truck was parked in front of the coffee
shop unloading new burlap bags of green coffee beans.

That could only mean one thing – roasting day!
The Neighborhood was going to smell great all afternoon.

Oakie ran ahead and barked for Sam to hurry up.
The sooner they finished their run through the
maze of sidewalks and alleys,
the sooner they could enjoy their coffee.

They ended their daily run at Parengo.

Sam ordered a yummy Mocha Latte and, as planned,
picked up a Salted Caramel Latte for Oakie.

Oakie watched the people while carefully licking the
frothy whipped cream off the top of his yummy coffee.

He thought about how lucky he was.
He had a warm bed, a great pal Sam, a sunny balcony to lay on,
plenty of squirrels to chase in the park across the street...

and a cool Coffee Shop that gave him coffee every day –
filling the neighborhood with amazing aromas.

He was happy the squirrels enjoyed acorns from the park.
He was glad the birds liked worms and bugs.
He was fine with the Cat eating goodies from the dumpster.
He was not ok with that sneaky mouse eating his dog food, which still made him grimace.

But Oakie...Oakie was simply a dog who loved coffee.

About the Author:

Camille Lancaster was inspired to write this story by the real-life Oakie who frequently visits her family's Downtown Coffee Shop in Southeast Missouri. She enjoys blogging at camillelancaster.com where she shares stories of her life with Jay and their 6 kids. Life is never boring at the Lancaster house.

About the Illustrator:

Emma Renfroe attends Missouri State University pursuing a career in Art Education. Constantly surrounding her self with art, she has learned that anyone can be an artist. There is art in everything we do!

CPSIA information can be obtained
at www.ICGtesting.com
Printed in the USA
BVHW010921251019
562014BV00008B/1/P